Sara Swan Miller

# Shorebirds

## From Stilts to Sanderlings

Franklin Watts - A Division of Grolier Publishing
New York • London • Hong Kong • Sydney • Danbury, Connecticut

*For Danny,*
*a "seabird" we'd like to see on shore more often*

Photographs ©: Animals Animals: 25 (Phyllis Greenberg); H. Armstrong Roberts, Inc.: 7 bottom (W. Metzen); Photo Researchers: cover (John W. Bova), 5 top left, 12, 13 (Tim Davis), 41 (François Gohier), 22, 23 (G. C. Kelly), 19 (Mark Newman), 15 (Rod Planck), 6 (David Weintraub), 27, 29 (Roger Wilmshurst), 43 top (Jim Zipp); Tom Vezo: 5 bottom right, 5 bottom left, 37; Visuals Unlimited: 21 (Gerald & Buff Corsi), 43 bottom (John D. Cunningham), 7 top, 39 (Barbara Gerlach), 1 (Gil López-Espina), 31 (Gary Meszaros), 5 top right, 42 (Arthur Morris), 17 (Kjell B. Sandved), 35 (Leroy Simon), 33 (Roger Treadwell).

Illustrations by Jose Gonzales and Steve Savage

The photograph on the cover shows a sanderling. The photo on the title page shows a roseate tern with a fish.

Visit Franklin Watts on the Internet at:
http://publishing.grolier.com

Library of Congress Cataloging-in-Publication Data

Miller, Sara Swan.
Shorebirds: from stilts to sanderlings / Sara Swan Miller.
  p. cm. — (Animals in order)
 Includes bibliographical references and index.
 Summary: Describes the general physical characteristics and behavior of shorebirds and takes an indepth look at fourteen different species.
 ISBN 0-531-11596-8 (lib. bdg.)       0-531-16498-5 (pbk.)
 1. Shorebirds—Juvenile literature. [1. Shorebirds.] I. Title. II. Series.
QL676.2.M565 2000
598.3′3—dc21              99-042009

# Contents

# Is That a Shorebird?

Have you ever watched a flock of noisy gulls fight over a scrap of food? Have you seen sandpipers patter back and forth at the edge of the beach? Maybe you've watched skimmers fly low over the ocean or puffins diving for fish.

These birds look and act differently from one another, but they all belong to the same group, or *order* of birds. This order is called charadriiformes (KAR-ah-dree-uh-FOR-meez), which means "plover-like birds." They certainly don't all look like plovers, though. People generally call birds in this group "shorebirds," even though they don't all live at the shore.

On the next page are four shorebirds. Each is quite different from the others. Can you guess why they are all placed in the same order?

Northern jacana

Atlantic puffin

Ring-billed gull

Sanderling

# Traits of Shorebirds

To understand why shorebirds are all in the same order, you would need X-ray vision. Scientists look at a bird's skeleton, the roof of its mouth, and how its feathers grow to decide whether it is a shorebird.

Scientists believe that all shorebirds have a common ancestor that lived millions of years ago. Over time, each kind of shorebird changed to suit its lifestyle. Shorebirds that spend a lot of time wading, such as stilts, developed long legs. Gulls, terns, and puffins have webbed feet that help them swim. Plovers and curlews don't need webbed feet because they spend their time on land. The jacana has very long toes that allow it to walk on top of water plants.

**A stilt's long legs make wading easy.**

Different shorebirds developed different kinds of *bills* too. A skimmer's lower bill is longer than its top bill. It ploughs the water with its lower bill as it hunts for fish. Oystercatchers have long, bladelike bills that are perfect for opening oyster shells. Puffins have large bills, so they can catch several fish at once. Other shorebirds use their long, thin bills to probe the sand for food.

**A puffin with four fish**

Most shorebirds have a few things in common though. Most mate for life, and many nest together in colonies. Many shorebirds make their nests on the ground. The *hatchlings* are covered with down, their eyes are open and alert, and their legs are well developed. Soon after they hatch, the young birds are able to run about, and many of them can feed themselves.

**A colony of royal terns**

# The Order of Living Things

A tiger has more in common with a house cat than with a daisy. A true bug is more like a butterfly than a jellyfish. Scientists arrange living things into groups based on how they look and how they act. A tiger and a house cat belong to the same group, but a daisy belongs to a different group.

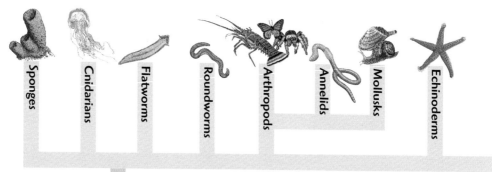

Sponges  Cnidarians  Flatworms  Roundworms  Arthropods  Annelids  Mollusks  Echinoderms

Animals

Plants  Fungi

Protists

Monerans

All living things can be placed in one of five groups called *kingdoms*: the plant kingdom, the animal kingdom, the fungus kingdom, the moneran kingdom, or the protist kingdom. You can probably name many of the creatures in the plant and animal kingdoms. The fungus kingdom includes mushrooms, yeasts, and molds. The moneran and protist kingdoms contain thousands of living things that are too small to see without a microscope.

8

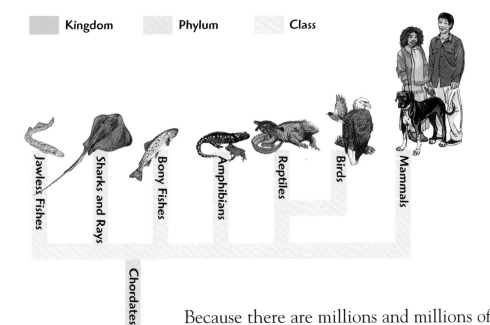

Kingdom   Phylum   Class

Jawless Fishes
Sharks and Rays
Bony Fishes
Amphibians
Reptiles
Birds
Mammals
Chordates

Because there are millions and millions of living things on Earth, some of the members of one kingdom may not seem all that similar. The animal kingdom includes creatures as different as tarantulas and trout, jellyfish and jaguars, salamanders and sparrows, elephants and earthworms.

To show that an elephant is more like a jaguar than an earthworm, scientists further separate the creatures in each kingdom into more specific groups. The animal kingdom can be divided into nine *phyla*. Humans belong to the chordate phylum. Almost all chordates have a backbone.

Each phylum can be subdivided into many *classes*. Humans, mice, and elephants all belong to the mammal class. Each class can be further divided into orders; orders into *families*, families into *genera*, and genera into *species*. All the members of a species are very similar.

# How Shorebirds Fit In

You can probably guess that shorebirds belong to the animal kingdom. They have much more in common with spiders and snakes than with maple trees and morning glories.

Shorebirds belong in the chordate phylum. Almost all chordates have a backbone and a skeleton. Can you think of other chordates? Examples include elephants, mice, snakes, frogs, fish, and whales.

All birds belong to the same class. There are about thirty different orders of birds. Shorebirds make up one of these orders.

Shorebirds are divided into a number of different families and genera. There are at least 150 species of shorebirds. Shorebirds live in almost every part of the world. You can find them on the beach, far out to sea, in meadows and marshes, in the woods, and even in your neighborhood landfill. In this book, you will learn more about fifteen different species of shorebirds.

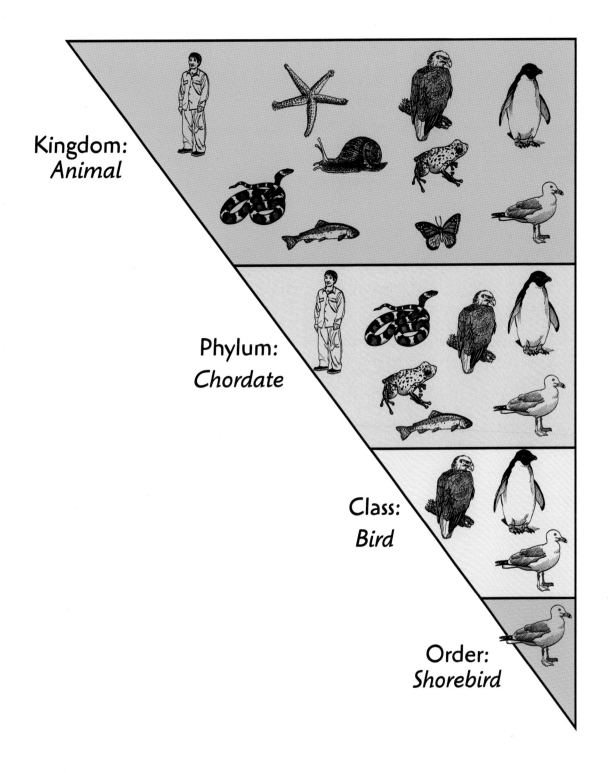

Kingdom:
*Animal*

Phylum:
*Chordate*

Class:
*Bird*

Order:
*Shorebird*

# Stilts

FAMILY: Recurvirostridae
COMMON EXAMPLE: Black-necked stilt
GENUS AND SPECIES: *Himantopus mexicanus*
SIZE: 13 to 16 inches (33 to 41 cm)

The black-necked stilt has a slim, elegant-looking body and is well suited to life in a marsh. It barely ruffles the water as it strides through the shallows on its long, thin legs. Its needlelike bill is perfect for picking insects and other small creatures off the water's surface.

Black-necked stilts may look fragile, but they are tough birds. You can see groups of stilts stalking about the edges of lakes and marshes or poking their bills into mud on the shore. They eat all kinds of insects, as well as shrimp, snails, and crayfish. Sometimes they snap up a tadpole or a tiny fish just below the water's surface. Every so often, they snatch an insect as it flies past.

Colonies of stilts build their nests on bare, open ground not far from the water.

12

Sometimes they build mounds above the waterline and place shells and pebbles inside. At other times, the birds lay their eggs in holes they have scraped out with their bills. When it gets too hot, adult black-necked stilts wet their belly feathers in the water and sit on the eggs to cool them down. Now that's instant air-conditioning!

# Gulls

**FAMILY:** Laridae
**COMMON EXAMPLE:** Ring-billed gull
**GENUS AND SPECIES:** *Larus delawarensis*
**SIZE:** 18 to 20 inches (46 to 51 cm)

More than fifty species of gulls live in the world, and to most people, they all look alike. You can almost always recognize a ring-billed gull, though. It has a black band around the tip of its yellow bill.

Like all gulls, ring-bills are noisy birds. Sometimes their high-pitched calls sound like screams, and sometimes the birds sound as though they're laughing. They build their nests in large colonies, usually on islands in lakes. One colony in Ontario, Canada, has 85,000 pairs of ring-billed gulls. You can imagine the racket!

When spring comes, males and females *court*. They stretch upright, face each other, turn away, and then face each other again. After a while, the male coughs up some food and offers it to the female. Maybe she likes getting a bill full of half-digested food. After the gulls mate, the female builds a messy nest of grass and sticks on the ground. Then she lays two to four eggs. Both parents feed the hatchlings until they can find their own food on the beach. Five weeks later, the young birds can finally fly.

Almost anywhere you go in North America—seashores, farmland, parking lots, or garbage dumps—you'll see plenty of ring-

billed gulls. What is the secret of their success? They eat almost any-
thing—insects, fish, worms, rodents, grain, and garbage. If there's
something to eat, ring-billed gulls will find it.

# Skimmers

FAMILY: Laridae
COMMON EXAMPLE: Black skimmer
GENUS AND SPECIES: *Rynchops niger*
SIZE: 18 inches (46 cm)

As dusk falls over the ocean, a black skimmer hunts for fish just under the water's surface. It flies swiftly just above the water with its beak open and its long lower jaw plowing through the water. When the skimmer finds its *prey*, the bird immediately snaps its bill shut and flies off with its catch.

The skimmer is the only bird with a bill that is longer on the bottom than on the top. It is an excellent tool for catching fish, especially at dusk when fish rise toward the surface. A skimmer also has special eyes with vertical *pupils*—narrow slits that cut down the glare from the sand and water.

Skimmers nest on beaches in large, noisy colonies. If you bother them, they get even noisier—yapping, screaming, and squawking harshly until you go away. Nest building is simple for skimmers. They just squat down in the loose sand and turn around and around to make a hole for their eggs.

The young start running about the beach in search of food when they're just 2 days old. At first, both parts of their bill are the same length. Their long lower bill develops at about the time that they learn to fly. Then they can set off over the ocean to hunt for fish.

# Oystercatchers

FAMILY: Haematopodidae
COMMON EXAMPLE: American oystercatcher
GENUS AND SPECIES: *Haematopus palliatus*
SIZE: 17 to 21 inches (43 to 53 cm)

You can probably guess what an oystercatcher likes to eat. That's right, oysters. They also feed on clams and mussels. To catch prey, an oystercatcher stalks slowly through shallow water, peering everywhere for an open oyster, clam, or mussel shell. When the bird spots one, it jabs its beak into the shell and cuts the animal's muscles before the prey can close its shell. Then the oystercatcher gulps down its meal.

An oystercatcher's bill is a perfect tool for nabbing oysters. It is long, hard, and flat on the top and bottom—like a knife, and it has a sharp tip—like a chisel. If an oystercatcher finds a closed shell, it may hammer on the shell with its chisel-like bill until the shell breaks open. Sometimes oystercatchers pry a *limpet*—a type of sea snail—off a rock, flip it over, and gobble it up.

In the spring, you may see male and female oystercatchers courting. First they walk along side by side. Then they begin running together and make loud piping calls. Finally, they fly up and away, still piping loudly. Once the birds have each other's full attention, they mate, and the female lays eggs.

Young oystercatchers leave the nest soon after they hatch. Their parents feed them for about 2 months, but then the young begin hunting for themselves.

# Killdeer

**FAMILY:** Charadriidae
**COMMON NAME:** Killdeer
**GENUS AND SPECIES:** *Charadrius vociferus*
**SIZE:** 9 to 11 inches (23 to 28 cm)

You might wonder how the killdeer got its name. After all, there's no way a bird could kill a deer. As these birds fly over open fields, they call out "Killdeer! Killdeer!" These birds were named for the sounds they make, not the food they eat.

Killdeer live in pastures and plowed fields, where they patter along hunting for beetles, caterpillars, grasshoppers, and other small insects. Killdeer often follow a farmer's plow and gobble up beetle grubs the plow brings to the surface. Many farmers are grateful that killdeer hang around their fields and eat grubs.

When spring comes, male killdeer fly high over nesting sites with slow, deep wing beats. They are trying to catch a female's attention and scare other males away. Killdeer nests are simple. The birds just scrape out a spot on the bare ground. Sometimes they line the nest with grass, twigs, and pebbles.

Killdeer are good parents. When the weather turns hot, they shade their nests with their outspread wings. When an enemy gets too close, one of the adults flutters along the ground away from the nest, holding its wing down as if it is broken. The *predator* sees easy prey and goes after it. Then the parent flies away, and the nest is saved.

# Jacanas

**FAMILY:** Jacanidae
**COMMON EXAMPLE:** Northern jacana
**GENUS AND SPECIES:** *Jacana spinosa*
**SIZE:** 8 to 9 inches (20 to 23 cm)

Is that bird walking on water? Almost! A jacana can run about on top of lily pads and other floating water plants because it has very long toes. Some people call jacanas "lily-trotters." The jacana feeds on insects living on or just below the water's surface. It also eats any small fish that it can catch.

The jacana doesn't fly often, but when it does, it usually flies slowly with its long legs dangling. After the jacana lands, it holds its wings up for a while.

In the spring, a male jacana makes a flimsy nest on a marsh plant and defends the area around it. Each female mates with as many as four males and lays eggs in each nest. Then the males settle down to sit on the eggs.

22

The female jacana doesn't have time to pay much attention to the eggs or the young. She is busy defending all of the nests. She uses the sharp spurs on her wings to fight off other birds. Many intruders probably think twice before doing battle with a fierce mother jacana.

# Avocets

**FAMILY:** Recurvirostridae
**COMMON EXAMPLE:** Pied avocet
**GENUS AND SPECIES:** *Recurvirostra avosetta*
**SIZE:** 17 inches (43 cm)

At the edge of a lagoon, a pied avocet swings its head from side to side and sweeps its long, up-curved bill through the shallow water. It is busy searching for water insects.

Sometimes the avocet stands perfectly still. When an insect comes near, the bird suddenly plucks its prey from the water. Now and then, an insect flies past and becomes a meal. Finally, the bird settles in the water and swims quickly along with webbed feet. Then it tips its body over and searches for small creatures under the water's surface. Avocets have developed all kinds of ways to find food.

In the spring, avocets nest in colonies. Males and females work together to build a nest. They scrape out a hole in the sand and line it with pebbles and grass that they find nearby. The male and female take turns sitting on the eggs.

If an enemy comes too close, the adults swing into action. They fly away from the nest and hobble about on the ground, pretending to have a broken wing. This usually lures the predator away from the nest. Meanwhile, other birds in the colony scream the alarm. Some may even dive down at the intruder's head.

# Curlews

**FAMILY:** Scolopacidae
**COMMON EXAMPLE:** Common curlew
**GENUS AND SPECIES:** *Numenius arquata*
**SIZE:** 20 to 24 inches (51 to 61 cm)

If you walk on a beach in winter, you may see common curlews strolling along the edge of the water. Every so often, the birds call out their soft, whistling "cur-lee."

As they walk slowly along, the curlews poke their long, curved bills deep into the sand, probing for worms and shellfish. If a curlew finds a crab, it breaks off the legs, crushes its shell, and swallows the meat.

In the spring, curlews *migrate* to peat bogs and grasslands. Curlews are not colorful birds, but you can't help but notice a male curlew when he courts a female. He flies into the air and makes a series of whistles that get faster and faster. As he swoops slowly down, the whistles become a lovely, bubbling trill.

The female seems to like the whistling. When the male curlew lands, the two call back and forth to let each other know they're interested in mating. Then the female chooses a dry, raised place on the ground to build a nest. She makes a hole and lines it with soft grass, *lichens*, and moss.

Both parents take care of the hatchlings, even after the young birds can feed themselves. In June, the female leaves, but the male stays with the young and continues to protect them from enemies.

# Lapwings

**FAMILY:** Charadriidae
**COMMON EXAMPLE:** Northern lapwing
**GENUS AND SPECIES:** *Vanellus vanellus*
**SIZE:** 12 inches (30 cm)

In the spring, the male northern lapwing is a real acrobat. He flies above his territory and tumbles over and over, all the while calling out "pee-oo-vit" and "wee-oo-way." As he flies, the wind rushes over his rounded wings and makes a loud humming sound. His crazy flight, striking colors, and long crest make him impossible to miss.

All this activity attracts females and drives other males away. After the birds mate, the female scrapes out a nest on the ground. She lines it with dry grass, pebbles, and whatever else she finds lying about.

It's easy to tell the difference between male and female lapwings. A female's colors are dull. She blends in with her surroundings, so it's hard for a predator to spot her as she sits on her eggs. Even though a male has brighter colors, he spends some time sitting on the eggs.

Lapwing chicks start looking for food soon after they hatch. You may see young lapwings hunting for food with their parents. These birds patter about in a field or marsh. When they spot an insect or worm, they run toward it, stop suddenly, snatch up the prey, and then run on again.

In the fall, northern lapwings fly south in big flocks. Their return is one of the first signs of spring.

29

# Snipes

**FAMILY:** Scolopacidae
**COMMON EXAMPLE:** Common snipe
**GENUS AND SPECIES:** *Gallinago gallinago*
**SIZE:** 10 inches (25 cm)

Out in a marsh, a common snipe hunts for dinner. The bird sticks its long bill into the mud and searches for insects, worms, and other small creatures. The tip of a snipe's bill is very sensitive. When it feels a worm under the mud, the bird quickly snaps up the prey. Then it searches for more good things to eat.

When a snipe senses danger, it crouches down. If it is in the water, only its back is visible. If it is in a field, the bird's colors help it blend with its surroundings. Either way, the snipe is hard to spot. If an enemy gets too close, the bird suddenly explodes from its hiding place and takes off. It flies in a zigzag pattern and calls out "Ketsch! Ketsch!" in a harsh voice. The predator is so startled that the snipe usually escapes.

In the spring, especially at dusk, the male flies in high circles and makes acrobatic dives. He is trying to attract a mate. As the wind rushes through the male's feathers, it makes an eerie drumming sound.

After the birds mate, the female builds a nest and lays her eggs. She sits on the eggs until they hatch. After the young snipes leave the nest, the male helps feed them. The parents split the *brood*, each taking care of only one or two young. This surely makes the job easier.

# Turnstones

FAMILY: Scolopacidae
COMMON EXAMPLE: Ruddy turnstone
GENUS AND SPECIES: *Arenaria interpres*
SIZE: 8 to 10 inches (20 to 25 cm)

It's easy to see how the ruddy turnstone got its name. It runs about on rocky beaches, flipping over stones with its chisel-like bill. The hungry little bird is looking for small creatures hiding underneath the rocks. When a stone is too large, several birds team up to turn it over.

Ruddy turnstones eat all kinds of things. In the winter, they eat crabs, barnacles, clams, mussels, worms, sea urchins, and small fish. In the summer, when they nest on the Arctic *tundra*, they eat insects, spiders, berries, seeds, and even moss. Turnstones also eat dead animals when they come across them and visit dumps to feed on food scraps. They puncture and eat other birds' eggs too.

Ruddy turnstones live in many different parts of the world. Why are these birds so successful? There are two reasons—they eat many different kinds of foods, and they build their nests in the far north, so very few enemies disturb them.

Female turnstones build nests on the ground, and both parents sit on the eggs. The female leaves soon after the young hatch, but the male stays and takes care of them.

# Sanderlings

FAMILY: Scolopacidae
COMMON NAME: Sanderling
GENUS AND SPECIES: *Calidris alba*
SIZE: 7 to 8 1/2 inches (18 to 22 cm)

Sanderlings look like little wind-up toys as they putter along the shore on their quick legs. When a wave draws back, they race down to the water's edge to probe for small creatures in the wet sand. When a new wave rolls to shore, they race up the beach again. These tireless little birds do this again and again as they search for food.

Sanderlings find lots of sand crabs, worms, and other creatures in the wet sand along the tide line. They also eat dead fish, horseshoe crab eggs, and even corn chips and other junk food people leave on the beach.

In the spring, they migrate to the Arctic tundra to raise their young. There they feed on flies and other insects, seeds, *algae*, and leaves. With such a varied diet, no wonder they can be found on beaches all over the world.

In the spring, the male sanderling lets out a harsh chirring song as he flutters and glides through the sky. Then he flies to the ground, runs up to a female, hunches his head down on his shoulders, and ruffles his feathers. All this showing off seems to please the female.

After the birds mate, the female makes two shallow nests in the ground—one for her and one for him. She lays eggs, and each bird sits on its nest. Soon after the chicks hatch, the female flies south. Fortunately, the young birds can fend for themselves.

# Jaegers

**FAMILY:** Laridae
**COMMON EXAMPLE:** Long-tailed jaeger
**GENUS AND SPECIES:** *Stercorarius longicaudus*
**SIZE:** 20 to 24 inches (51 to 61 cm)

Unless you are on a boat out in the open ocean, you may never see a jaeger. Except at mating time, jaegers spend most of their lives flying over the water in search of fish. They even sleep on the waves.

Jaegers are graceful birds. They soar upward or hover over the water looking for food. They can pluck fish out of the water as they hover. They also follow fishing boats and wait for people to throw unwanted fish overboard. Jaegers are pirates too. If a jaeger sees a gull or tern catch a fish, it will attack the other bird and try to steal the prey.

In the spring, adult jaegers migrate to the Arctic tundra to mate. They nest in noisy colonies, and defend their nest sites ferociously. If an enemy appears, they raise both wings, stick out their necks, and scream harshly until the intruder backs off.

Young jaegers leave the nest soon after they hatch, but they stay nearby. The female guards them while the male hunts for large insects or small mammals called lemmings. When he comes back, he throws up what he has eaten, and everyone has a feast. In about 6 weeks, the young can fly. They will spend the next 7 or 8 years at sea before returning to land to raise a family of their own.

# Terns

**FAMILY:** Laridae
**COMMON EXAMPLE:** Common tern
**GENUS AND SPECIES:** *Sterna hirundo*
**SIZE:** 13 to 16 inches (33 to 41 cm)

A female tern swoops over the water, just above the crashing waves. She peers at the water below, slows, and hovers over the surface. Suddenly, she plunges into the water and pops up with a slippery fish clamped in her bill. A male tern sees the dangling fish. He chases the female and tries to steal her meal. She's too fast for him, though, and flies away to enjoy her meal in peace.

During the mating season, however, males are much nicer to females. A male will fly over a group of females, carrying a fish in his bill. Soon a female flies along after him. When the birds land, they bow to each other and strut in circles. Finally, the male bows to the female one last time and offers her the fish. This may convince her that he'll be a good provider.

The young leave the nest a couple of days after they hatch. Because the hatchlings can't fly, the parents continue to bring them fish, shrimp, and other small animals. A few weeks later, the young learn to catch their own fish.

Common terns aren't as common as they once were. Until the end of the nineteenth century, people hunted them for their feathers. Finally, laws were passed to protect terns.

# Puffins

**FAMILY:** Alcidae
**COMMON EXAMPLE:** Atlantic puffin
**GENUS AND SPECIES:** *Fratercula arctica*
**SIZE:** 11 1/2 to 13 1/2 inches (29 to 34 cm)

Puffins look and act like clowns. They buzz about with their gaudy bills pointing the way and their red, webbed feet spread out behind. Those colorful bills earned them the nickname "sea parrot."

If a puffin comes up from a dive and finds a boat nearby, it seems to lose its head. It doesn't know what to do. It dips its head underwater as if it's going to dive, then seems to change its mind and starts to fly. Then it suddenly dives through a wave, comes out the other side, and dives again. Finally, it manages to blunder its way to safety.

These odd-looking birds are serious hunters, though. They dive down into the cold ocean water and race after fish. To catch their prey, they paddle with their feet and steer with their wings. These strong little swimmers can dive up to 200 feet (61 m) deep, and they can hold as many as 30 wiggling fish in their beaks at once!

Puffins are serious about parenting too. They dig a long burrow to nest in and take turns sitting in the dark tunnel for 5 to 7 weeks. After their only egg hatches, the parents feed their hungry chick for up to 7 weeks. Finally, one night, the young bird flies off to sea.

# Watching Shorebirds

People all over the world enjoy bird-watching. Would you like to get to know shorebirds better and have fun at the same time?

You'll probably want a pair of binoculars. Most birders like 10 × 40 field glasses. They make a bird look ten times larger. You'll also want a field guide to help you identify the birds you see. Field guides show pictures of birds and describe each bird's field marks—features that are easy to see from far away. Field marks include size and color, the shape and color of the bill, and certain colors and markings on feathers.

Most birders keep a notebook. It is a good place to keep track of when and where you see shorebirds and to write down how they behave. You can even draw pictures in your notebook.

**This boy is watching a group of gulls.**

Sandpipers, gulls, and terns are among the easiest shorebirds to watch. At the seashore, you'll usually spot at least a few of these birds. When you see one, keep your eyes on it while you raise your binoculars. Then take a good look at the bird. How big is it? What color are its feathers? What special markings does it have? Check your field guide to see whether you can find out what kind of shorebird it is. Many of them look similar, so look carefully.

It's fun to learn the names of different birds, but it's more interesting to watch how different birds behave. What do they eat? How do they find food? Do they try to steal other birds' food? In the spring, look for birds courting. Do you see birds bobbing or strutting around each other? Do you see a male offer a fish to a female? What else do you notice? Draw pictures and write down everything you observe. The more you watch and listen for shorebirds, the more you'll learn about them.

**A common tern**

**A gull with a crab**

# Words to Know

**alga** (plural **algae**)—a tiny green plantlike creature

**bill**—a hard, pointed structure on a bird's face; it acts as a bird's nose and mouth

**brood**—a group of young birds born at the same time to the same parents

**court**—to behave in a way that will attract a member of the opposite sex for mating

**class**—a group of creatures within a phylum that share certain characteristics

**family**—a group of creatures within an order that share certain characteristics

**genus** (plural **genera**)—a group of creatures within a family that share certain characteristics

**hatchling**—an animal that has recently hatched from an egg

**kingdom**—one of the five divisions into which all living things are placed: the animal kingdom, the plant kingdom, the fungus kingdom, the moneran kingdom, and the protist kingdom

**lichen**—a living thing that consists of a fungus and an alga

**limpet**—a marine creature with a low, cone-shaped shell that sticks itself to rocks or timbers

**migrate**—to travel to a different location to find food or reproduce

**order**—a group of creatures within a class that share certain characteristics

**phylum** (plural **phyla**)—a group of animals within a kingdom that share certain characteristics

**pupil**—the part of the eye that controls how much light enters

**predator**—an animal that hunts and eats other animals

**prey**—an animal that is hunted and eaten by another animal

**species**—a group of creatures within a genus that share certain characteristics. Members of the same species can mate and produce young.

**tundra**—a treeless, frozen plain in northern Arctic regions

# Learning More

## Books

Kress, Stephen W., *Project Puffin: How We Brought Puffins Back to Egg Rock*. Gardiner, ME: Tilbury House Publishers, 1997.

Latimer, Joseph P., Karen Stray Nolting, and Roger Tory Peterson. *Peterson Field Guides for Young Naturalists: Shorebirds*. Boston: Houghton Mifflin, 1999.

Miller, Debbie S., and Daniel Van Zyle. *Flight of the Golden Plover: The Amazing Migration Between Hawaii and Alaska*. Portland, OR: Alaska Northwest Books, 1996.

Rupp, Rebecca, and Jeffrey C. Domm. *Everything You Never Learned About Birds: Lore & Legends*. Pownal, VT: Storey Publishing, 1995.

Taylor, Barbara, and Richard Orr. *Bird Atlas*. London: DK Publishing, 1993.

## Web Sites

### Cornell Laboratory of Ornithology
*http://www.ornith.cornell.edu*
This site offers students the opportunity to participate in an on-line BirdWatch project. It also features a bird of the week, other bird projects, and information about how people can help protect the world's birds.

### The Shorebird Watcher
*http://www.netcom.com/~djhoff/shorbrd.html*
This site has lots of links, photos, scientific information, and a section that takes you to sites where you can listen to the calls of shorebirds.

# Index

# About the Author

**Sara Swan Miller** has enjoyed working with children all her life, first as a nursery-school teacher, and later as an outdoor environmental educator at the Mohonk Preserve in New Paltz, New York. As the director of the Preserve school program, she has led hundreds of children on field trips and taught them the importance of appreciating and respecting the natural world.

She has written a number of children's books, including *Three Stories You Can Read to Your Dog*; *Three Stories You Can Read to Your Cat*; *What's in the Woods? An Outdoor Activity Book*; *Oh, Cats of Camp Rabbitbone!*; *Piggy in the Parlor and Other Tales*; *Better Than TV*; and *Will You Sting Me? Will You Bite? The Truth About Some Scary-Looking Insects*. She has also written many other books for the Animals in Order series as well as several books about farm animals for the Children's Press True Books series.